THE CIVIL WAR

RECONSTRUCTION

by Olivia Ghafoerkhan

FOCUS
READERS.

VOYAGER

www.focusreaders.com

Focus Readers is distributed by North Star Editions:
sales@northstareditions.com | 888-417-0195

Produced for Focus Readers by Red Line Editorial.

Content Consultant: Dr. Gideon Mailer, Associate Professor of History, University of Minnesota Duluth

Photographs ©: Everett Historical/Shutterstock Images, cover, 1, 4–5, 7, 13, 19, 25, 33; World History Archive/Newscom, 8–9; James F. Gibson/Library of Congress, 11; Brady-Handy Photograph Collection/Library of Congress, 14–15, 31, 43; Red Line Editorial, 17, 23, 28; Thomas Nast/Library of Congress, 20–21; Circa Images/Glasshouse Images/Alamy, 26–27, 45; Wallach Division Picture Collection/New York Public Library, 34–35; Mathew B. Brady/Library of Congress, 37; State of Louisiana/Wikimedia Commons, 38; Library of Congress, 40–41

Library of Congress Cataloging-in-Publication Data
Names: Ghafoerkhan, Olivia, 1982- author.
Title: Reconstruction / Olivia Ghafoerkhan.
Description: Lake Elmo, MN : Focus Readers, [2020] | Series: The Civil War
 | Includes bibliographical references and index. | Audience: Grades 7-9
Identifiers: LCCN 2019035468 (print) | LCCN 2019035469 (ebook) | ISBN
 9781644930830 (hardcover) | ISBN 9781644931622 (paperback) | ISBN
 9781644933206 (pdf) | ISBN 9781644932414 (ebook)
Subjects: LCSH: Reconstruction (U.S. history, 1865-1877)--Juvenile
 literature. | Southern States--History--1865-1877--Juvenile literature.
Classification: LCC E668 .G39 2020 (print) | LCC E668 (ebook) | DDC
 973.8--dc23
LC record available at https://lccn.loc.gov/2019035468
LC ebook record available at https://lccn.loc.gov/2019035469

Printed in the United States of America
Mankato, MN
012020

ABOUT THE AUTHOR

Olivia Ghafoerkhan is an author of nonfiction books. She lives in Northern Virginia close to Washington, DC. She earned her MFA from Hamline University. She teaches English at a community college. Learning the history of the places around her has always been a favorite pastime.

TABLE OF CONTENTS

CHAPTER 1

RESHAPING THE NATION

On April 11, 1865, Abraham Lincoln stepped onto the White House lawn. The US president gave a speech as a crowd listened. Lincoln began with talk of victory. The Civil War (1861–1865) had split the nation in half. Eleven states in the South had formally left the Union. These states didn't want the **federal** government to prevent slavery from expanding. Instead, they believed each state should be allowed to choose for itself.

Abraham Lincoln gives a speech during his second inauguration on March 4, 1865.

So, they broke off to form a separate country. They called it the Confederate States of America.

Many Northerners wanted to bring the Southern states back into the Union. By early 1865, the Confederates seemed likely to lose the war. People debated what should happen afterward. What process should the states follow to rejoin the Union? And how much control should the federal government have over them?

Democrats tended to oppose federal control of the Southern states. Before the war, many Democrats supported slavery. If the Confederates lost, enslaved people would become free. But most Democrats didn't want that to happen.

Radical Republicans disagreed. They believed black people should have equal rights as **citizens**. They wanted the federal government to make and enforce this change.

Lincoln was shot while attending a play at Ford's Theatre in Washington, DC.

Lincoln was a moderate Republican. He believed slavery was wrong. But he also believed in balancing the desires of states and the power of the federal government. When the war began, Lincoln had no plans to end slavery. By April 1865, however, that had changed. Lincoln spoke in favor of free black men having the right to vote. He promised to announce a new plan for the South. Then, on April 14, an assassin shot Lincoln. The president died the next day. His plan would never come to pass.

EMANCIPATION

Proclamation

Whereas on the 22d day of September in the year of our Lord 1862 a Proclamation was issued by the President of the United States containing among other things the following to wit

That on the first day of January in the year of our Lord 1863 all persons held as slaves within any State or designated part of a State the people whereof shall then be in rebellion against the United States, shall be then thenceforth and forever free and the Executive Government of the United States, including the military and naval authority thereof will recognize and maintain the freedom of such persons and will do no act or acts to repress such persons or any of them in any effort they may make for their actual freedom.

That the Executive will on the first day of January aforesaid by proclamation designate the States and parts of States if any in which the people therein respectively shall then be in rebellion against the United States, and the fact that any State or the people thereof shall on that day be in good faith represented in the Congress of the United States by members chosen thereto at elections wherein a majority of the qualified voters of such State shall have participated, shall in the absence of strong countervailing testimony be deemed conclusive evidence that such State and the people thereof are not then in rebellion against the United States.

NOW THEREFORE I
ABRAHAM LINCOLN
PRESIDENT of the UNITED STATES
BY VIRTUE OF THE POWER IN ME VESTED AS
COMMANDER IN CHIEF of the ARMY and NAVY

in time of actual armed rebellion against the authority and government of the United States and as a fit and necessary war measure for suppressing said rebellion do on this first day of January in the year of our Lord one thousand eight hundred and sixty three, and in accordance with my purpose so to do publicly proclaimed for the full period of one hundred days from the day of the first above mentioned order and designate as the States and parts of States wherein the people thereof respectively are this day in rebellion against the United States the following to wit Arkansas Texas Louisiana except the parishes of St Bernard Plaquemines Jefferson St John St Charles St James Ascension Assumption Terre Bonne Lafourche St Mary St Martin and Orleans including the City of New Orleans Mississippi Alabama Florida Georgia South Carolina North Carolina and Virginia except the forty eight counties designated as West Virginia and also the counties of Berkeley Accomac North ampton Elizabeth City York Princess Ann and Norfolk including the cities of Norfolk and Portsmouth and which excepted parts are for the present left precisely as if this proclamation were not issued And by virtue of the power and for the purpose aforesaid I do order and declare that all persons held as slaves within said designated States and parts of States are and henceforward shall be free, and that the executive government of the United States including the military and naval authorities thereof will recognize and maintain the freedom of said persons. And I hereby enjoin upon the people so declared to be free to abstain from all violence unless in necessary self defense and I recommend to them that in all cases when allowed, they labor faithfully for reasonable wages And I further declare and make known that such persons of suitable condition will be received into the armed service of the United States to garrison forts positions stations and other places and to man vessels of all sorts in said service And upon this sincerely believed to be an act of justice warranted by the Constitution upon military necessity, I invoke the considerate judgment of mankind and the gracious favor of Almighty God In witness whereof I have hereunto set my hand and caused the seal of the United States to be affixed Done at the city of Washington this first day of January in the year of our Lord one thousand eight hundred and sixty three and of the independence of the United States of America the eighty seventh.

A Lincoln

CHAPTER 2

FREE AND EQUAL

Lincoln's 1865 speech wasn't his first effort to end slavery in the South. In 1863, he issued the Emancipation Proclamation. It freed enslaved people in areas fighting for the Confederacy. But a few Union states still allowed slavery.

The official end to slavery came after the Civil War. The Thirteenth Amendment changed the US Constitution to make slavery illegal throughout the country. Congress passed it in January 1865.

The Emancipation Proclamation took effect in January 1863.

But for the amendment to take effect, two-thirds of the states had to **ratify** it.

In the meantime, lawmakers began plans to help formerly enslaved people after the war. In March 1865, Congress created the Freedmen's Bureau. This government agency helped newly freed black people. It also helped many white people who had lost their homes during the war. The Bureau gave people food and clothing. It tried to help them get land as well.

During the war, people in the South often fled approaching armies, leaving their land and property behind. In addition, the Confiscation Act allowed Union troops to take the property of people who supported the Confederacy. Soldiers seized homes, fields, and plantations throughout the South. They often forced the owners to leave and gave the land to freed black people.

▲ Union troops used this house in Fair Oaks, Virginia, as a hospital.

By 1865, Union forces had confiscated more than 750,000 acres (303,500 hectares) of land.

Lawmakers argued about what to do with this land. Southern planters wanted their land back. They wanted to keep growing tobacco, cotton, and other crops on large farms. Radical Republicans disagreed. They wanted to rent or sell the land to recently freed black people. They planned to divide the large farms into small sections.

The Freedmen's Bureau planned to rent these sections to poor people. After three years, the Bureau hoped the renters would be able to buy the land. However, legal conflict meant most leases were only temporary. White people still owned most of the land in the South.

Even so, the Bureau supported black Americans in other ways. One was education. Many people saw school as a key step toward equality and freedom. People who could read, write, and do math could get better jobs. These skills also helped people avoid unfair labor contracts.

➤ THINK ABOUT IT

Learning to read and write helped people avoid unfair labor contracts. How else can education help people improve their quality of life?

In the 1800s, some black Americans took classes at freedmen's colleges.

Planting and harvesting crops took lots of hard work. For centuries, plantations had forced enslaved workers to provide free labor. After slavery was abolished, planters had to pay their workers. Some planters treated black workers almost like slaves. But the Bureau worked to help black workers get better contracts and wages.

Churches also played a key role in equality. After the war, independent black churches sprang up all across the South. They would become places of political action in the coming years.

CHAPTER 3

PRESIDENTIAL RECONSTRUCTION

After Lincoln's death in April 1865, Andrew Johnson took office. Johnson had been Lincoln's vice president. He was a Democrat. Like Lincoln, he wanted to make it easy for states to rejoin the Union. But compared to Lincoln, Johnson thought states should have greater freedom to govern themselves. He believed each state should be able to do as it wished after ratifying the Thirteenth Amendment.

Andrew Johnson was the 17th president of the United States.

Johnson wanted to help Southerners rebuild. He offered pardons to many Confederates. A pardon is official forgiveness for a crime. Leaving the Union and starting a war was an act of treason, which is the crime of betraying a country. As a result, people who sided with the Confederacy were considered criminals. They couldn't get their land back. They also couldn't vote or run for office.

A pardon forgave this crime and restored the person's rights. To be pardoned, people had to swear a loyalty oath. They promised to obey the laws of the United States and be loyal to the government. By 1866, Johnson had issued more than 7,000 pardons.

Johnson also set up **interim** governments in Southern states. Congress was not in session during the summer of 1865. The lawmakers were on break until December. But Johnson wanted the states to rejoin the Union before then. So, he told the Southern states to hold meetings to elect new leaders. Each state's leaders would then create a new government.

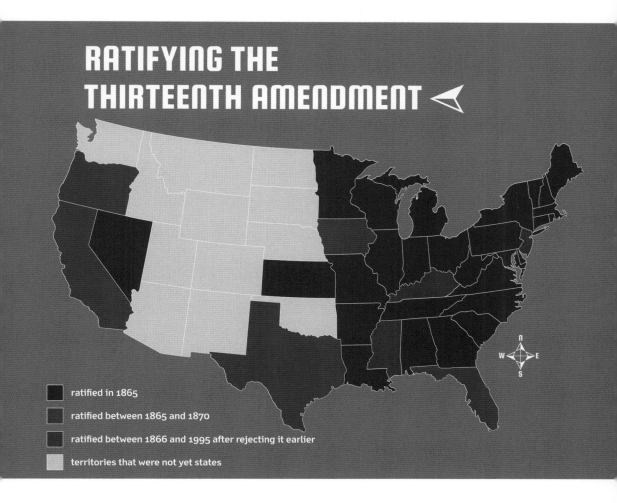

RATIFYING THE
THIRTEENTH AMENDMENT ◁

ratified in 1865

ratified between 1865 and 1870

ratified between 1866 and 1995 after rejecting it earlier

territories that were not yet states

Over the next few months, Southern states ratified the Thirteenth Amendment and selected their leaders. Most of the leaders they chose were white men who owned property. Many had even been leaders of the Confederacy. As a result, the new governments worked to keep the South much like it had been before the war. Many passed laws known as Black Codes. These laws limited the rights of black people.

The laws said black people could only work as farmhands or house servants. Black workers had to sign written contracts. Any black person without a work contract could be arrested, fined, and put in jail. And anyone who couldn't pay the fine had to work off the debt, often in a job that paid very little. Other laws allowed courts to take children away from their parents and put them in **apprenticeships**. By the end of 1865, conditions

Throughout the 1860s, people held conventions to support the rights of black people.

for black people in the South were nearly as bad as they had been under slavery.

Throughout the fall and winter, events known as colored conventions took place all over the South. These gatherings focused on improving conditions and gaining equal rights for black people. People met in churches and schools. They spoke about the conditions in the South. And they asked lawmakers to protect their rights.

WHAT THEY WERE.

ANDREW JOHNSON'S
RECONSTRUCTION,

MEMPHIS.   NEW-ORLEANS.

TREASON IS A
CRIME AND MUST BE
MADE ODIOUS, AND TRAITORS
MUST BE PUNISHED

LOVE THINE
ENEMIES

I AM YOUR
MOSES
TO LE

JOHNSON. VETOS
FREEDMEN'S BURE
CIVIL RIGHTS BILL
AND THE
AMENDMENT TO THE U.S.
CONSTITUTION

Dr. P. B. RANDOLPH A COLORED MAN
HAD DINNER AND A GRATEFUL
GLASS OF WINE AT THE WHITE
HOUSE.
SEE N.Y. TIM

I AM ONE
OF YOUR
BEST
FRIENDS

A. JOHNSON'S

PLANTATION BATTE

Good FOR THE
CONSTITUTION

HONORABLE DISCHARGE

U.S. GRANT

OTHELLO. DOST THOU MOCK ME?

IAGO.   I MOCK YOU! NO, BY HEAVEN:
WOULD YOU WOULD BEAR YOUR FORTUNES LIKE A MAN.
SHAKSPEARE.

1862.

VETOES
AND
PARDONS
TO BE
HAD HERE

NORTH PRO

CHAPTER 4

REPUBLICANS REACT

When Congress met again in December 1865, Republicans refused to accept the South's new leaders. At the time, the Republican Party held most of the seats in Congress. Most members of this party hoped to keep Confederate leaders from regaining power. They also wanted to protect the rights of black people in the South. For example, on December 13, Congress formed the Joint Committee on Reconstruction.

A political cartoon by Thomas Nast criticizes President Johnson's plans for Reconstruction.

This group would investigate conditions in Southern states. Republicans in Congress also passed a **civil rights** bill. They expanded the Freedmen's Bureau, too. It would now apply to black people all over the country, not just in the South. Johnson vetoed both bills. But both times, Congress voted to override his veto. The lawmakers got the required two-thirds majority, and both bills became law.

Next, Republicans in Congress drafted the Fourteenth Amendment. It protected the rights of former slaves. Its text stated that anyone born in the United States was a US citizen. States would be punished if they did not give black male citizens the right to vote. The text also said former Confederate leaders could not hold office. Congress passed the amendment in June 1866. Then it went on to the states.

That same month, the Joint Committee on Reconstruction gave its report to Congress. It found that Southern states had created a system much like slavery. Republicans decided it was time for the federal government to get involved.

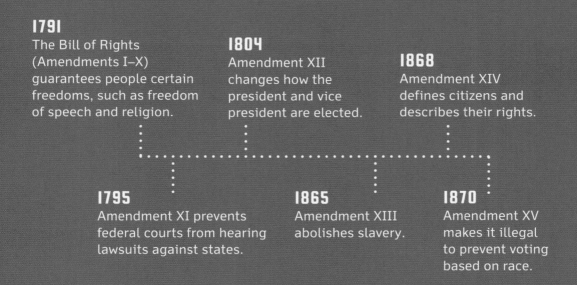

CONSTITUTIONAL AMENDMENTS ◀

By the end of the 1800s, the states had ratified 15 amendments to the US Constitution.

1791
The Bill of Rights (Amendments I–X) guarantees people certain freedoms, such as freedom of speech and religion.

1804
Amendment XII changes how the president and vice president are elected.

1868
Amendment XIV defines citizens and describes their rights.

1795
Amendment XI prevents federal courts from hearing lawsuits against states.

1865
Amendment XIII abolishes slavery.

1870
Amendment XV makes it illegal to prevent voting based on race.

SUSAN B. ANTHONY

Many people hoped the Fourteenth Amendment would say women had the right to vote. Activists such as Susan B. Anthony wrote to Congress. However, many lawmakers didn't think women should be allowed to vote. Including women's rights could make the amendment unpopular. Leaders worried it wouldn't get enough votes to pass. So, they left that part out.

Even so, Anthony believed that the Fourteenth Amendment applied to women. The amendment stated that all US citizens have certain rights. A citizen is a person born in the United States. In a speech in 1873, Anthony used a question to make her point. "Are women persons?"[1] she asked. The obvious answer was yes. "Being persons," Anthony argued, "women are citizens."[2] And as citizens, women should have all the same rights as men.

Susan B. Anthony was a leading advocate for women's right to vote.

At the time, some state laws prevented women from voting, holding political office, and owning property. But Anthony claimed that "every discrimination against women" was "null and void."[3] She said the laws went against the Fourteenth Amendment. Lawmakers disagreed. They said that was not what the amendment meant. Several decades would pass before women finally gained the right to vote.

1. Lynn Sherr. *Failure Is Impossible: Susan B. Anthony in Her Own Words*. New York: Times Books, 1995. 112.
2. Sherr. *Failure Is Impossible*. 112.
3. Sherr. *Failure Is Impossible*. 112.

CHAPTER 5

RADICAL RECONSTRUCTION

Starting in March 1867, Congress passed four Reconstruction acts. These laws divided the South into five military districts. Officers from the US Army were in charge of each district. These officials organized elections to create new state governments. First, each state elected **delegates** for a constitutional convention. At this convention, the delegates wrote new laws for the state. Next, voters ratified the new constitution.

Radical Reconstruction focused on providing equal rights for black Americans.

27

But before it became law, the US Congress had to approve it, too. Finally, the state had to ratify the Fourteenth Amendment. At that point, the state would be allowed back into the Union. This plan became known as Radical Reconstruction.

Johnson thought Congress should not tell state governments what to do. So, he vetoed all four

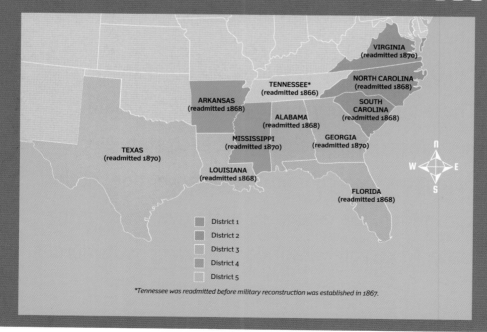

STATES AND DISTRICTS IN THE SOUTH

VIRGINIA
(readmitted 1870)

NORTH CAROLINA
(readmitted 1868)

TENNESSEE*
(readmitted 1866)

SOUTH
CAROLINA
(readmitted 1868)

ARKANSAS
(readmitted 1868)

ALABAMA
(readmitted 1868)

GEORGIA
(readmitted 1870)

MISSISSIPPI
(readmitted 1870)

TEXAS
(readmitted 1870)

LOUISIANA
(readmitted 1868)

FLORIDA
(readmitted 1868)

District 1
District 2
District 3
District 4
District 5

*Tennessee was readmitted before military reconstruction was established in 1867.

Reconstruction acts. Each time, Congress voted to overturn his veto. The House of Representatives also accused Johnson of obstruction, the crime of stopping or slowing the process of the law. Its members voted to **impeach** him in 1868.

The case went to the Senate next. Most senators opposed Johnson's actions. But they weren't sure he had committed a crime. Plus, they worried that removing him from office would give the House too much power. As a result, the Senate voted to acquit Johnson, declaring him not guilty.

Meanwhile, the new state governments created changes in the South. In the past, most lawmakers had been rich white men. Now, more black men and poor white men were able to vote. These new voters elected people who shared their ideas and backgrounds. Nearly one-fourth of delegates for the constitutional conventions were black men.

The new state constitutions gave all male citizens the right to vote, no matter their skin color. They also changed tax laws to no longer favor the rich. In addition, states began offering free education for all children. Before this, the South had no system of public education. People had to pay to attend private schools.

Radical Republicans won state elections across the South in 1867 and 1868. Thousands of black leaders were elected to state and local political offices. And in the years that followed, 16 black men became members of Congress.

However, Republicans knew these gains could be reversed. States might change their laws and constitutions to prevent black people from voting. To keep this from happening, Congress created the Fifteenth Amendment. The amendment said states could not deny a person's right to vote

▲ In 1870, Joseph Rainey became the first black man to serve in the US House of Representatives.

because of race. But states could still make people take tests or pay taxes in order to vote. Some states would later use these methods to stop black voters.

By 1870, all 11 Southern states had met the requirements of Radical Reconstruction and rejoined the Union. And in February 1870, the states ratified the Fifteenth Amendment.

HIRAM REVELS

Hiram Revels was the first black man to serve in the US Senate. He was born free in North Carolina in 1827. He studied theology and became a minister. After the Civil War, Revels settled in Mississippi. In January 1870, he won a seat representing the state in Congress.

Revels was a moderate Republican. He thought anyone "in the South who gives evidence that he is a loyal man"[1] should have all rights restored. This included the rights to vote and hold office. It even applied to Confederate leaders. Revels gave a speech to Congress describing this view. He said the Republican party was "wide enough for all truly loyal men."[2]

Revels also wanted all people to have access to education. He opposed **segregation**. In fact, he believed racism would fade if the laws that supported it were gone. "Let lawmakers cease

△ Hiram Revels was one of two black senators elected during Reconstruction.

to make the difference," he wrote, "and the people will soon forget it."[3] If laws no longer kept students separated by race, Revels thought people would treat one another equally.

Revels served in the Senate for just over a year. Then he returned to Mississippi. He became the first president of Alcorn University. This school was one of the first colleges for black students.

1. *Black Congressmen During Reconstruction: A Documentary Sourcebook.* Edited by Stephen Middleton. Westport, CT: Greenwood Publishing Group, 2002. 327.
2. *Black Congressmen.* 323.
3. *Black Congressmen.* 332.

CHAPTER 6

SHIFTING GROUND

Some people resisted the changes in the South. A major opponent was the Ku Klux Klan (KKK). This group used violence and intimidation to stop Republican voters, especially black people. KKK members attacked and killed Republican leaders. They also targeted schools and churches.

Congress tried to stop the violence by passing a series of laws. These laws allowed the federal government to take action to keep elections fair.

Democrats in the South worked to restrict the voting rights of black Americans.

One example was the Ku Klux Klan Act. This law gave the federal government power to send troops and officials to oversee state and local elections in cases involving the KKK.

By the late 1860s, the Republican Party was shifting away from radical reform. However, moderate Republicans remained in favor of Reconstruction. They supported Ulysses S. Grant, who became president in 1869. Grant supported efforts to stop violence in the South. But other radical ideas began losing support. For example, the redistribution of land and wealth was growing unpopular. This shift was tied to business.

> ## ➤ THINK ABOUT IT

Besides targeting schools and churches, the KKK often attacked teachers. Why do you think they did this?

▲ Ulysses S. Grant had been a general in the US Army during the Civil War.

Some people in the North grew rich by owning businesses and property. Like Southern planters, business owners tended to oppose unions and workers' rights. Republicans began putting less emphasis on making social changes. Instead, they focused on helping businesses.

By Grant's second term, support for civil rights was fading. Many Northerners had been opposed to slavery. But few wanted full racial equality.

STATE OF LOUISIANA--PARISH OF JEFFERSON

Office of Sheriff and Tax Collector.

_____ 19___

Received of _A. S. White_

resident of _Second_ (2) Ward, the sum of ONE DOLLAR, Poll Tax

the year 191 _2_, for the support of the PUBLIC SCHOOLS.

Louis L. Barenhan

Sheriff and Ex-Officio Tax

▲ Poll taxes made it difficult for black citizens to vote.

Several states passed segregation laws. And while
the Fifteenth Amendment granted voting rights
to black men, loopholes remained. For example,
Delaware passed a poll tax in 1873. It required all
people to pay a certain amount of money to vote.
Rich people could easily pay. But the majority of
black people were poor. Many could not afford to
pay the tax. As a result, they were unable to vote.

That same year, several court cases shifted how
the Fourteenth Amendment was enforced. The

cases questioned which rights the amendment protected. The Supreme Court ruled that civil rights were not included. The court said it didn't want to give the federal government too much control over states. But this decision limited the amendment's power to protect black citizens. States would not be forced to follow the new civil rights laws.

A **depression** in 1873 weakened support for Reconstruction even more. Some people even blamed Reconstruction for causing the depression. All the laws and programs cost lots of money to enforce. People throughout the country had to pay taxes to fund them. Many Northerners saw these taxes as an unfair burden. They were tired of trying to solve the South's ongoing problems. They thought the South should solve them on its own.

CHAPTER 7

THE END OF AN ERA

In the 1870s, Democratic leaders in the South came up with a plan to regain control of the region. They focused on the 1875 elections in Mississippi. The leaders created a strategy to win majorities in the state's government.

First, they tried to scare white people in the state into voting for Democrats. At the time, elections used open ballots. That meant anyone could see which candidates each voter chose.

By the end of the 1800s, many black families worked as sharecroppers on Southern farms.

Democrats looked up people who voted for Republicans. They threatened these voters or forced them to leave the area.

Second, Democrats worked to keep black people in Mississippi from voting. They used threats and violence. Many black voters stayed home. They feared losing their jobs, their homes, or their lives.

Mississippi's governor worried that the election would turn violent. He asked President Grant to send federal troops to keep peace. Grant refused. He said this was an issue states should handle on their own. In December 1874, riots broke out

> ## ➤ THINK ABOUT IT

President Grant chose not to send troops to keep peace in Vicksburg. Do you agree with his decision? Why or why not?

In the hotly debated election of 1876, both sides accused the other of fraud. Rutherford B. Hayes barely won.

in the city of Vicksburg. Two white citizens and 29 black citizens died. Still, Grant did not send federal troops.

Democrats used similar tactics in other states. Their party won many elections throughout the South. But it was the presidential election of 1876 that ended Reconstruction completely. Republican Rutherford B. Hayes won the election by a very narrow margin. As president, Hayes promised not to interfere in the politics of the Southern states.

Soon, many states passed Jim Crow laws. These laws separated people by race. They limited where black people could live, work, shop, and go to school. The laws also gave black workers fewer rights.

Other laws kept black people from voting. Because of the Fifteenth Amendment, none of these laws actually said black people couldn't vote. But the laws made it extremely hard for them to do so. Some laws required black people to take complex reading tests. Other laws charged expensive poll taxes.

By the late 1800s, black Americans again faced inequalities in many areas of life. Many worked as sharecroppers. They farmed land owned by someone else. In return, they gave that person a share of their profit. Land owners charged high prices for supplies but gave low pay. Many black

⬛ Students attend a school in South Carolina.

families became trapped in a cycle of debt. Some worked on the same farms where their families had been enslaved.

The one lasting change was public education. Reconstruction laws helped provide education for all children. Before the war, school was available only to people with money to pay for it. But after the war, public education was free. This change paved the way for future progress.

FOCUS ON
RECONSTRUCTION

Write your answers on a separate piece of paper.

1. Write a paragraph summarizing the main ideas of Chapter 3.

2. Do you think the House of Representatives was right to impeach President Johnson? Why or why not?

3. Which amendment officially ended slavery?
   - **A.** the Thirteenth Amendment
   - **B.** the Fourteenth Amendment
   - **C.** the Fifteenth Amendment

4. What might have happened if Democratic candidates had not won so many elections in the 1870s?
   - **A.** The changes of Reconstruction might have focused more on white workers in the North.
   - **B.** The changes of Reconstruction might never have been passed by Congress.
   - **C.** The changes of Reconstruction might not have been reversed so quickly.

Answer key on page 48.

GLOSSARY

apprenticeships
Positions where young people learn a trade and receive low wages in return for their work.

citizens
People who legally belong to a certain country and have specific rights as a result.

civil rights
Rights that protect people's freedom and equality.

delegates
People who are selected to vote, act, or speak on behalf of others.

depression
A period of time when an area's economy struggles, prices rise, and people lose their jobs.

federal
Having to do with the top level of government, involving the whole nation rather than just one state.

impeach
To bring formal charges against someone serving in office to determine if that person is guilty of a crime.

interim
Temporary; existing only until an official or long-term version replaces it.

ratify
To formally approve a law, treaty, or amendment by voting.

segregation
The separation of groups of people based on race or other factors.

TO LEARN MORE

BOOKS

Hamen, Susan E. *Civil War Aftermath and Reconstruction.* Minneapolis: Abdo Publishing, 2017.

LaPierre, Yvette. *Living Through the Civil War.* Vero Beach, FL: Rourke Educational Media, 2019.

Uhl, Xina M., and Timothy Flanagan. *A Primary Source Investigation of Reconstruction.* New York: Rosen Central, 2019.

NOTE TO EDUCATORS

Visit **www.focusreaders.com** to find lesson plans, activities, links, and other resources related to this title.

INDEX

Answer Key: 1. Answers will vary; **2.** Answers will vary; **3.** A; **4.** C